1821   CENSUS

Hartfield

Sussex

Transcribed and published by
PBN Publications

1989

Published by
PBN Publications
22 Abbey Road
Eastbourne
Sussex BN20 8TE

Reproduced in microfiche 2001

Introduction by C.R.Davey, B.A.
County Records Officer
East Sussex Record Office

i

INTRODUCTION

The 1821 Census

Census returns have been taken every ten years since 1801, but while statistical information from them is available in printed form (and often in papers preserved among parish records as well), lists of the names of inhabitants were not preserved nationally until 1841. In a few cases, however, lists were preserved locally, either as drafts, or as copies. Mostly these were of heads of households, rather than full population listings, and they are to be found among overseers' papers surviving among parish records. The purpose of these publications is to publish the lists which survive for East Sussex for the census taken on 28 May 1821.

The two local parishes for which lists of persons survive to be reproduced in this series are Chiddingly and Hartfield. Both exist in small notebooks preserved among the parish records in the East Sussex Record Office - Chiddingly as PAR292/37/1, and Hartfield as PAR360/15/2/1. That for Hartfield is the more typical of those which survive for this early period - it is essentially a list of householders with numbers of males and females in each household, though the nature of the family occupation is indicated, and sometimes the name of the wife and (occasionally) of other members of the family.

The Chiddingly return is more unusual. For a start it
lists all inhabitants with their ages and relationships;
but it also has extensive annotations giving subsequent
details of death or other information although this
additional information is not included in this publication.
It is thus of some interest and importance.

A number of other parishes have information from the
census, but no names. Other parishes have population
totals noted on the flyleaf of the parish register. For a
full history of the Census and of the information required
in successive returns, see the Guide to Census Reports:
Great Britain: 1801-1966 by the Office of Population,
Census and Surveys (HMSO, 1977).

Roger Davey, County Records Officer.

ACKNOWLEDGMENT

PBN Publications wish to acknowledge the help and advice
given by Mr. C.R. Davey - County Records Officer - East
Sussex Record Office and for permission to publish this
list.

ABBREVIATIONS

FAM	Number of Families resident in that house
FEM	Number of Females
HOU	Houses
Jun	Junior
MAL	Number of Males
Sen	Senior
UN	Uninhabited building
Yrs	Years

The names listed in this publication are taken as written on the copies from which this was transcribed.

Further copies may be obtained from 22 Abbey Road, Eastbourne, Sussex. BN20 8TE. Send S.A.E. for details please.

SURNAMES IN THIS PUBLICATION

ABBOT,ANDERSON,ANDRESS,ATHERFOLD,ATKINS,ATTREE,BACHELOR,BAILY,BAKER,BAL-
DWIN,BARRETT,BARTON,BASHFORD,BENNETT,BENTLY,BISHOPP,BOURNER,BRADFORD,
BRIDGER,BRISSENDEN,BRITT,BROOKER,BROWN,BUCKMAN,BUCKWELL,BURR,BUTCHER,CAM-
BRIDGE,CARD,CARDEN,CARPENTERCHAPMAN,CHART,CHEAL,COOPER,CORD,COUPER,COX,
CREASEY,CROUCH,CROWHURST,DADSWELL,DANIEL,DIVALL,DORRY,DOWNARD,EARLE,EAST,
EDWARDS,EGGINS,ELLIOTT,ELLIS,EVEREST,EVES,FETHERSTONE,FILLERY,FITNESS,
FOSTER,FOX,FROST,FRY,FULLER,GAINSFORD,GARRETT,GASSON,GIBB,GODLY,GOODWIN,
GORRINGE,GURNEY,HALE,HALL,HANNAKER,HARMER,HATFIELD,HAWKINS,HESMAN,HEVERS,
HEWARD,HEWETT,HILLER,HILLS,HOLLAMBY,HOLLINGDALE,HOLMES,HOOKER,HORSEY,HUG-
GETT,HUHON,HUMPHREY,HUMPHRY,HUTSON,ILLMAN,INKPIN,JARRETT,JENKINS,JENNER,
JINKS,KENWARD,KIDD,KILNER,KNIGHT,LANGRIDGE,LEIGH,LENEY,LINDFIELD,LOCK,
LUCAS,LUCK,MARDEN,MAY,MEADS,MEDHURST,MERCER,MILES,MILLS,MITCHELL,MOLE,
MOON,MORPHEW,MUGGRIDGE,NEWTON,NORMAN,NUGENT,OUNSTEAD,OUNSTED,PAINE,
PAINLY,PANKHURST,PARKHURST,PARTRIDGE,PAWLEY,PERVEY,PHILCOX,PIPER,PRIT-
CHETT,PURLIP,RALPH,READ,RICHARDSON,ROBERTS,ROGERS,RUSSELL,RYE,SADLER,
SALES,SANDALLS,SEAL,SEALE,SENDALLS,SHAW,SHERBORNE,SHOOBRIDGE,SHOOSMITH,
SIMMONS,SLADE,SLATER,SMITH,SOPFORTH,SPENCER,STILLER,STREATFIELD,TASKER,
THORP,THORPE,TIDY,TODMAN,TOWN,TRILL,TURK,TURNER,UNDERWOOD,WAGHORN,WALLIS,
WATERS,WATKINS,WATSON,WEBB,WELFARE,WELLER,WESTON,WHATLEY,WHEATLEY,WICKEN,
WICKENS,WICKIN,WICKS,WILLS,WINDING,WINNIFRITH,WINNIFRITHS,WOODHOUSE,WREN,
YOUNG.